Program Authors

Diane August

Donald R. Bear

Janice A. Dole

Jana Echevarria

Douglas Fisher

David Francis

Vicki Gibson

Jan Hasbrouck

Margaret Kilgo

Jay McTighe

Scott G. Paris

Timothy Shanahan

Josefina V. Tinajero

McGraw Hill Education

Cover and Title pages: Nathan Love

www.mheonline.com/readingwonders

Copyright © 2017 McGraw-Hill Education

Send all inquiries to:
McGraw-Hill Education
2 Penn Plaza
New York, NY 10121

ISBN: 978-0-07-679825-4
MHID: 0-07-679825-9

Printed in the United States of America.

2 3 4 5 6 7 8 9 RMN 20 19 18 17 16

A

Unit 9 How Things Change

The Big Idea: How do things change?

(t) Camila De Godoy; (c) Chris Vallo; (b) Ariel Skelley/Corbis

Essential Question
How can you help out at home?

Go Digital!

Helping Out!

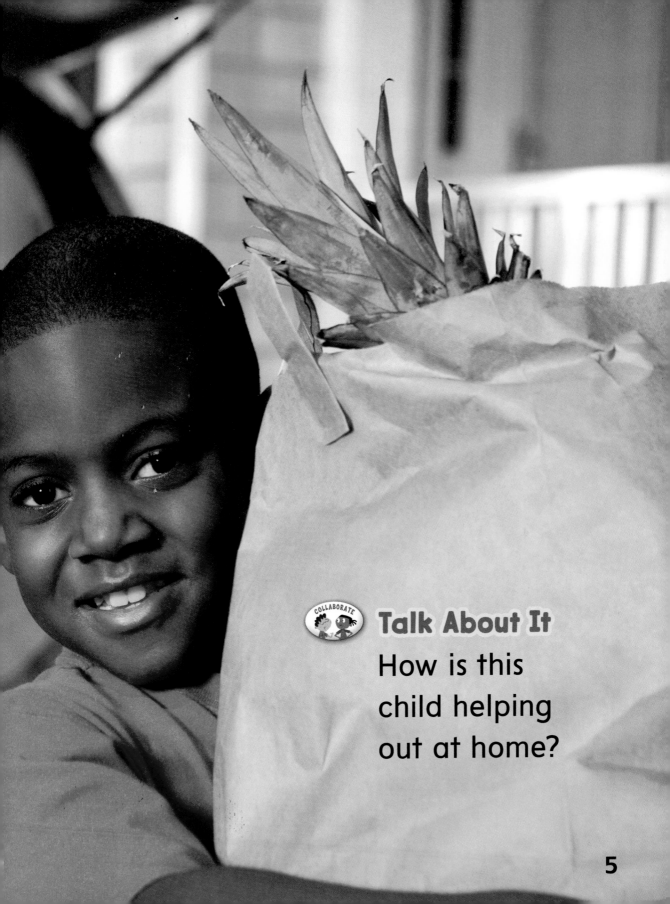

Talk About It

How is this child helping out at home?

Say the name of each picture.

Read each word.

3. **ate**   **safe**   **fame**

4. **bake**   **make**   **rate**

help	too

I **help** to rake the leaves.

Jake can help, **too**.

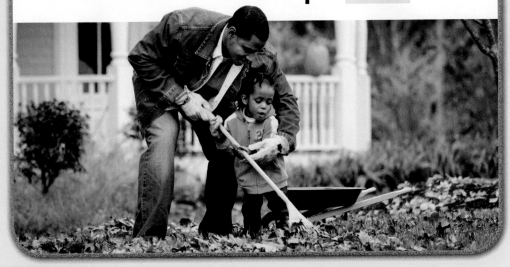

Jake and Dale Help!

Jake and Dale wake up.

Jake can make a bed.

Dale can make a bed, **too**.

"Can you **help**?" said Dad.
Dale can get a tan cup.
Jake can get the red jam.

Jake can take Rex.
Dale can take Rex, too.
Run, run Rex to the lake!

Jake and Dale help Dad.
Jake can wax a big van.
Dale can rake, rake, rake!

Camila de Godoy

Dale and Jake help Mom.
They get in a big van.
A big van can go, go, go!

Mom can get a big, big sack.
Dale can get a big yam.
Jake can get a cake mix.

Jake, Dale, and Mom bake.
They can bake a quick cake.
Dale and Jake help a lot!

Camila de Godoy

Write About the Text

Jake and Dale Help!

Jake and Dale woke up.
Jake can make a bed.
Dale can make a bed, too.

Pages 8-15

Marta

I responded to the prompt:
Write a journal entry as Jake describing how he felt about the things he did during the day.

Student Model: *Narrative Text*

Clues
I used the picture to figure out how Jake might have felt.

I liked to make my bed.
It made me feel like I was taking care of my things.
I felt good when I helped.
I felt like I was a big part of things.

16

Complete Sentences

My sentences tell complete ideas.

I wanted to make a delicious cake.

So, I picked out the cake mix.

I felt happy when I helped.

I felt like I was growing up!

Grammar

The word **delicious** is an **adjective**.

Your Turn

COLLABORATE

Write a journal entry as Dad describing how he felt about how Dale and Jake helped.

Go Digital!
Write your response online.
Use your editing checklist.

17

Weekly Concept Good Citizens

Essential Question

What do good citizens do?

Go Digital!

We Care!

Talk About It

How are these children being good citizens?

Radius Images/Alamy

Say the name of each picture.

1

2

Read each word.

3   **dime**   **mile**   **side**

4   **pipe**   **wipe**   **pine**

play	has

Mike and I **play** a game.

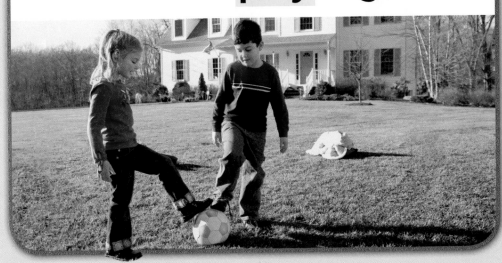

My class **has** a pet.

We Can Play

Chris Vallo

Mike can ride a red bike.
Kate can ride a tan bike.
They ride in a bike lane.

Chris Vallo

Mike is in a line.
Mike can let Pam in.
Pam can get in the line.

Pam can lick a red pop.

Mike can lick a lime pop.

Kate can get a big cup.

Chris Vallo

Mike **has** a fine red bike.
"It is mine," said Mike.
"But Pam can take a ride!"

Kate and Pam have a kite.
It can go up, up a mile!
Mike can let it go up, too.

Chris Vallo

Kate and Pam **play** a game.
They run a lot and kick.
The game is quite fun!

Pam can see Mike.
"You can play," said Pam.
They have a fun time.

Write About the Text

We Can Play

Mike can ride a red bike.
Kate can ride a tan bike.
They ride in a bike lane.

Pages 22–29

Jerome

I answered the questions: **How are Kate, Pam, and Mike the same? How are they different?**

Student Model: *Informative Text*

Kate, Pam, and Mike are the same in some ways. They all like the park. They like ice cream treats. They like to fly an orange kite. They all play soccer together. They all have lots of fun!

Grammar
The word **orange** is an **adjective.**

Imgorthand/iStock/Getty Images Plus/Getty Images

Specific Words

I used the word **older** to tell how Kate is different from Mike and Pam.

Kate, Pam, and Mike are also different. Mike and Kate ride their bikes. Pam does not. Pam and Mike lick pops. Kate eats from a big cup. Kate is older than Mike and Pam.

Order

I used text evidence to tell about the order of events in the story.

Your Turn

Describe how the children in this story play together. Are they good citizens? Why or why not?

Go Digital!
Write your response online.
Use your editing checklist.

31

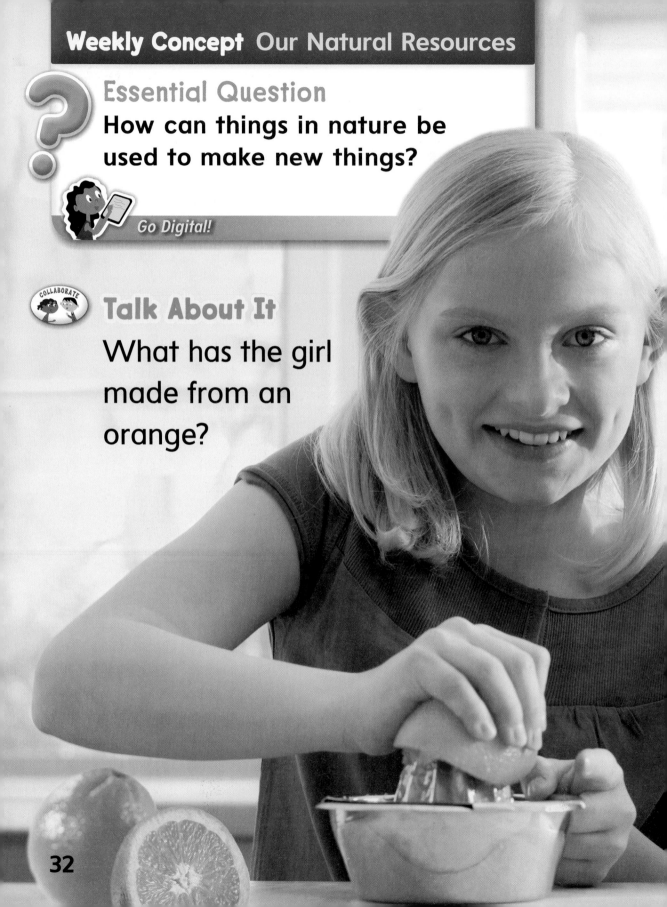

Essential Question

How can things in nature be used to make new things?

Go Digital!

COLLABORATE

Talk About It

What has the girl made from an orange?

The Wonders of Nature!

o   oa   ow

o_e   _oe

Say the name of each picture.

1

2

Read each word.

3   joke   hose   home

4   cone   hope   vote

where

look

Where do the roses grow?

Look at the owl's home.

(t)Mike Turner/Botanica/Getty Images; (b)NPS Photo by Willis Peterson

35

Look! A Home!

Look! Look!

It is quite a big site.

You can make a home.

37

Where can a pet go?
Can it go in a hole? No. No.
You can make Rose a
home.

Cole can sit in a fine home.
Cole can bite a big bone.
Yum! Yum! Yum! Yum!

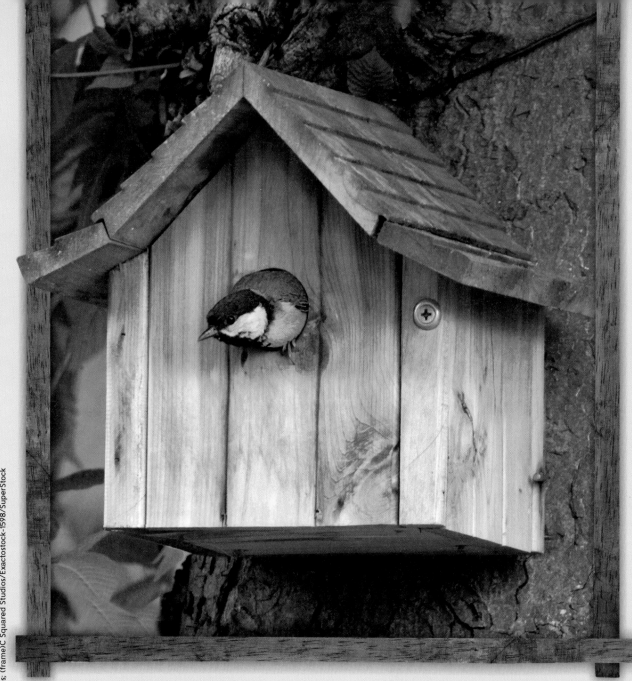

This is not a pet.
But we can make it a home.
It is safe in a home!

This is quite fine, too.
It is on a big, big pole.
I bet you can make it.

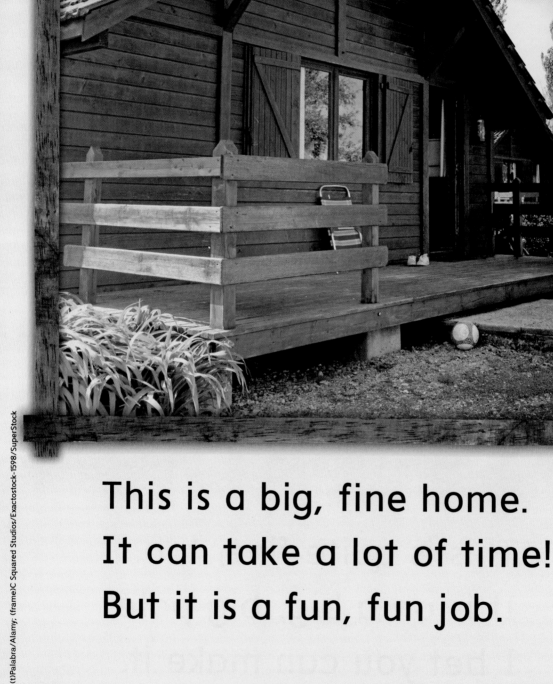

This is a big, fine home.
It can take a lot of time!
But it is a fun, fun job.

Look what you can make!
Sit on it and go up, up, up.
You can have a lot of fun.
I hope you like it!

Write About the Text

Pages 36–43

Ahmed

I responded to the prompt:
Compare the big house on page 37 to the bird house on page 40.

Student Model: *Informative Text*

Topic
I told about the home people can live in.

The big house will have many windows. It will also have a big door. It will have a big roof, too. It will be a big home. A lot of people can live there.

Facts
I used evidence to tell about the bird's home.

This bird's home is not big. A bird's home does not have windows. It has a small hole for the bird to go in and out. Both kinds of homes will keep people and birds safe.

Grammar
The word **small** is an **adjective.**

COLLABORATE

Your Turn
Have the girl tell in a journal entry how the homes on pages 38, 41, and 42 are alike and different.

Go Digital!
Write your response online.
Use your editing checklist.

45